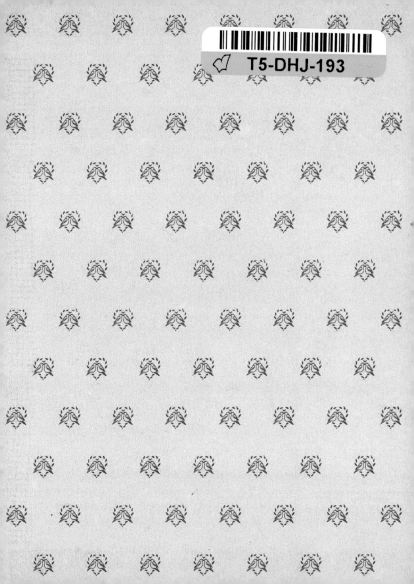
T5-DHJ-193

♑ LOVE SIGNS ♑

CAPRICORN

December 22 – January 20

JULIA & DEREK PARKER

Dedicated to Martin Lethbridge

A DK PUBLISHING BOOK

Project Editor • Annabel Morgan
Art Editor • Anna Benjamin
Managing Editor • Francis Ritter
Managing Art Editor • Derek Coombes
DTP Designer • Cressida Joyce
Production Controller • Martin Croshaw
US Editor • Constance M. Robinson

ACKNOWLEDGMENTS

Photography: Steve Gorton: pp. 10, 13–15, 17–19, 46–49; Ian O'Leary: 16. *Additional photography by:* Colin Keates, David King, Monique Le Luhandre, David Murray, Tim Ridley, Clive Streeter, Harry Taylor, Matthew Ward. *Artworks:* Nic Demin: 34–45; Peter Lawman: *jacket,* 4, 12; Paul Redgrave: 24–33; Satwinder Sehmi: *glyphs;* Jane Thomson: *borders;* Rosemary Woods: 11.

Peter Lawman's paintings are exhibited by the Portal Gallery Ltd, London.

Picture credits: Bridgeman Art Library/Hermitage, St. Petersburg: 51; Robert Harding Picture Library: 20l, 20c, 20r; Images Colour Library: 9; The National Gallery, London: 11; Tony Stone Images: 21t, 21b; The Victoria and Albert Museum, London: 5; Zefa: 21c.

First American Edition, 1996
2 4 6 8 10 9 7 5 3 1

Published in the United States by
DK Publishing, Inc., 95 Madison Avenue, New York, New York 10016
Visit us on the World Wide Web at http://www.dk.com

A catalog record is available from the Library of Congress.

ISBN 0-7894-1086-9

Reproduced by Bright Arts, Hong Kong
Printed and bound by Imago, Hong Kong

CONTENTS

ASTROLOGY & YOU

THERE IS MUCH MORE TO ASTROLOGY THAN YOUR SUN SIGN.
A SIMPLE INVESTIGATION INTO THE POSITION OF THE OTHER
PLANETS AT THE MOMENT OF YOUR BIRTH WILL PROVIDE YOU
WITH FASCINATING INSIGHTS INTO YOUR PERSONALITY.

*Y*our birth sign, or Sun sign, is the sign of the zodiac that the Sun occupied at the moment of your birth. The majority of books on astrology concentrate only on explaining the relevance of the Sun signs. This is a simple form of astrology that can provide you with some interesting but rather general information about you and your personality. In this book, we take you a step further, and reveal how the planets Venus and Mars work in association with your Sun sign to influence your attitudes toward romance and sexuality.

In order to gain a detailed insight into your personality, a "natal" horoscope, or birth chart, is necessary. This details the position of all the planets in our solar system at the moment of your birth, not just the position of the Sun. Just as the Sun occupied one of the 12 zodiac signs when you were born, perhaps making you "a Geminian" or "a Sagittarian," so each of the other planets occupied a certain sign. Each planet governs a different area of your personality, and the planets Venus and Mars are responsible for your attitudes toward love and sex, respectively.

For example, if you are a Sun-sign Sagittarian, according to the attributes of the sign you should be a dynamic, freedom-loving character. However, if Venus occupied Libra when you were born, you may make a passive and clinging partner – qualities that are supposedly completely alien to Sagittarians.

A MAP OF THE CONSTELLATION

*The 16th-century astronomer Copernicus first made the
revolutionary suggestion that the planets orbit the Sun
rather than Earth. In this 17th-century constellation chart,
the Sun is shown at the center of the solar system.*

The tables on pages 52–61 of
this book will enable you to
discover the positions of Mars
and Venus at the moment of
your birth. Once you have read
this information, turn to pages
22–45. On these pages we
explain how the influences of
Venus and Mars interact with
the characteristics of your
Sun sign. This information
will provide you with many
illuminating insights into your
personality, and explains how
the planets have formed your
attitudes toward love and sex.

LOOKING FOR A LOVER

ASTROLOGY CAN PROVIDE YOU WITH VALUABLE INFORMATION
ON HOW TO INITIATE AND MAINTAIN RELATIONSHIPS. IT CAN
ALSO TELL YOU HOW COMPATIBLE YOU ARE WITH YOUR LOVER,
AND HOW SUCCESSFUL YOUR RELATIONSHIP IS LIKELY TO BE.

*P*eople frequently use astrology to lead into a relationship, and "What sign are you?" is often used as a conversation opener. Some people simply introduce the subject as an opening gambit, while others place great importance on this question and its answer.

Astrology can affect the way you think and behave when you are in love. It can also provide you with fascinating information about your lovers and your relationships. Astrology cannot tell you who to fall in love with or who to avoid, but it can offer you some very helpful advice.

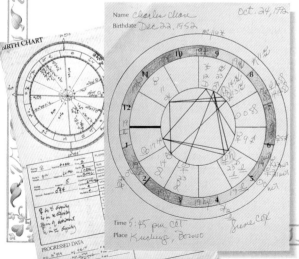

BIRTH CHARTS
*Synastry involves
the comparison
of two people's
charts in order
to assess their
compatibility in
all areas of their
relationship.
The process can
highlight any
areas of common
interest or
potential conflict.*

THE TABLE OF ELEMENTS

People whose signs are grouped under the same element tend to find it easy to fall into a happy relationship. The groupings are:

FIRE: *Aries, Leo, Sagittarius*
EARTH: *Taurus, Virgo, Capricorn*
AIR: *Gemini, Libra, Aquarius*
WATER: *Cancer, Scorpio, Pisces*

When you meet someone to whom you are attracted, astrology can provide you with a valuable insight into his or her personality. It may even reveal unattractive characteristics that your prospective partner is trying to conceal.

Astrologers are often asked to advise lovers involved in an ongoing relationship, or people who are contemplating a love affair. This important aspect of astrology is called synastry, and involves comparing the birth charts of the two people concerned. Each birth chart records the exact position of the planets at the moment and place of a person's birth.

By interpreting each chart separately, then comparing them, an astrologer can assess the compatibility of any two people, showing where problems may arise in their relationship, and where strong bonds will form.

One of the greatest astrological myths is that people of some signs are not compatible with people of certain other signs. This is completely untrue. Whatever your Sun sign, you can have a happy relationship with a person of any other sign.

YOU & YOUR LOVER

KNOWING ABOUT YOURSELF AND YOUR LOVER IS THE KEY TO
A HAPPY RELATIONSHIP. HERE WE REVEAL THE TRADITIONAL
ASSOCIATIONS OF CAPRICORN, YOUR COMPATIBILITY WITH ALL
THE SUN SIGNS, AND THE FLOWERS LINKED WITH EACH SIGN.

PINE AND
ELM TREES ARE
GOVERNED BY
THE SIGN OF
CAPRICORN

SATURN IS THE
RULING PLANET
OF CAPRICORN

THE CORNFLOWER
IS A CAPRICORN
HERB

SUBDUED DARK
GRAY AND
BROWN ARE
THE COLORS
MOST FREQUENTLY
ASSOCIATED
WITH CAPRICORN

CAPRICORNS
TEND TO BE TALL
AND THIN WITH
ELEGANTLY
SHAPED LEGS

GOATS AND OTHER
CLOVEN-HOOFED
ANIMALS FALL
UNDER THE
RULERSHIP
OF CAPRICORN

CAPRICORN AND ARIES
Arien exuberance may irritate you, because you like people to take life seriously. However, Aries will warm your cool heart, and your good sense will encourage Ariens to look before they leap.

Lavender is a Geminian flower

Thistles are ruled by Aries

CAPRICORN AND TAURUS
An earthy, sensual combination. You will find Taurean steadiness and tenacity attractive, and Taureans will admire your good sense. You are both very serious – remember to have a little fun.

The rose is associated with Taurus

CAPRICORN AND GEMINI
Flighty Geminians may be a little too lighthearted and frivolous for you. However, you will find their vivacity appealing, and Geminians will admire your humor and abundant energy.

The lily, and other white flowers, are ruled by Cancer

CAPRICORN AND CANCER
This is the classic attraction of opposites. Cancerians love domestic life, while Capricorns tend to be workaholics. You greatly admire and respect each other, and are a perfect pair.

CAPRICORN AND LEO

You two have much in common. You are both ambitious and demand a high standard of living. Leos will bring color and life to your cool personality, and you will bring them down to earth.

Hydrangeas are governed by Libra

Sunflowers are ruled by Leo

CAPRICORN AND LIBRA

The romantic and seductive charms of Libra will sweep you off your feet. Librans revel in the luxuries of life, and you will work hard to keep them in the style to which they are accustomed.

CAPRICORN AND VIRGO

You are well suited, but you may both devote too much of your time and energy to work. Try to set aside some time for leisure. Two earth signs guarantee a sensual and rewarding sex life.

Honeysuckle is attributed to Scorpio

Small, brightly colored flowers are associated with Virgo

CAPRICORN AND SCORPIO

Your cool and calm Capricorn personality has little in common with the deep passions of Scorpio. Give Scorpios constant assurance of your love, or they could become jealous and resentful.

CAPRICORN AND SAGITTARIUS
Carefree Sagittarians and pessimistic Capricorns are very different. However, if you overcome your differences, you could form a very rewarding, happy, and enduring attachment.

Orchids are associated with Aquarius

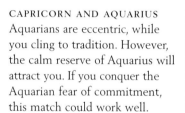

Carnations are ruled by Sagittarius

CAPRICORN AND AQUARIUS
Aquarians are eccentric, while you cling to tradition. However, the calm reserve of Aquarius will attract you. If you conquer the Aquarian fear of commitment, this match could work well.

CAPRICORN AND CAPRICORN
When two Capricorns get together, they will form a stable and successful alliance. Do not devote too much time to your work. Save some energy for relaxation and amusement.

Viburnum is governed by Pisces

Pansies are Capricorn flowers

CAPRICORN AND PISCES
Your reliability and steadiness will make insecure Pisceans feel protected, while you will be seduced by their powerful emotions. This is potentially an extremely successful union.

THE FOOD OF LOVE

WHEN PLANNING A SEDUCTION, THE SENSUOUS DELIGHTS OF AN
EXQUISITE MEAL SHOULD NEVER BE UNDERESTIMATED. READ ON
TO DISCOVER THE PERFECT MEAL FOR EACH OF THE SUN SIGNS,
GUARANTEED TO AROUSE INTEREST AND STIR DESIRE.

*Elaborate
confections
such as
pineapple
Pavlova will
appeal to a
Capricorn lover.*

– THE FOOD OF LOVE –

FOR ARIENS
Spicy mulligatawny soup
·
Peppered steak
·
Baked Alaska

FOR TAUREANS
Cream of cauliflower soup
·
Tournedos Rossini
·
Rich chocolate and brandy mousse

FOR GEMINIANS
Seafood and avocado salad
·
Piquant stir-fried pork with ginger
·
Zabaglione

FOR CANCERIANS
Artichoke vinaigrette
·
Sole Bonne Femme
·
Almond soufflé

– THE FOOD OF LOVE –

FOR LEOS
Roasted tomato and garlic soup
·
Boeuf Stroganoff
·
Pears cooked in wine

FOR VIRGOS
Eggplant salad
·
Paella
·
French apple tart

FOR LIBRANS
Asparagus with hollandaise sauce
·
Pork with roasted apples
·
Strawberry Pavlova

FOR SCORPIOS
Vichyssoise
·
Lobster Newburg
·
Blueberry cream

- THE FOOD OF LOVE -

FOR SAGITTARIANS
Chilled cucumber soup
·
Nutty onion flan
·
Rhubarb crumble with fresh cream

FOR CAPRICORNS
Eggs Florentine
·
Pork tenderloin stuffed with sage
·
Pineapple Pavlova

FOR AQUARIANS
Watercress soup
·
Chicken cooked with chili and lime
·
Lemon soufflé

FOR PISCEANS
French onion soup
·
Trout au vin rosé
·
Melon sorbet

PLACES TO LOVE

ONCE YOU HAVE WON YOUR LOVER'S HEART, A ROMANTIC
VACATION TOGETHER WILL SEAL YOUR LOVE. HERE, YOU
CAN DISCOVER THE PERFECT DESTINATION FOR EACH SUN
SIGN, FROM HISTORIC CITIES TO IDYLLIC BEACHES.

THE
EIFFEL
TOWER,
PARIS

ARIES

*Florence is an Arien
city, and its perfectly
preserved Renaissance
palaces and churches
will set the scene for
wonderful romance.*

TAURUS

*The unspoiled scenery
and unhurried pace
of life in rural Ireland
is sure to appeal to
patient and placid
Taureans.*

GEMINI

*Vivacious and restless
Geminians will feel at
home in the fast-paced
and sophisticated
atmosphere of
New York.*

CANCER

*The watery beauty
and uniquely romantic
atmosphere of Venice
is guaranteed to arouse
passion and stir the
Cancerian imagination.*

ST. BASIL'S
CATHEDRAL,
MOSCOW

AYERS ROCK/ULURU,
AUSTRALIA

LEO
Leos will fall in love all over again when surrounded by the picturesque charm and unspoiled medieval atmosphere of Prague.

VIRGO
Perhaps the most elegant and romantic of all cities, Paris is certainly the ideal setting for a stylish and fastidious Virgo.

LIBRA
The dramatic and exotic beauty of Upper Egypt and the Nile will provide the perfect backdrop for wooing a romantic Libran.

SCORPIO
Intense and passionate Scorpios will be strongly attracted by the whiff of danger present in the exotic atmosphere of New Orleans.

SAGITTARIUS
The wide-ranging spaces of the Australian outback will appeal to the Sagittarian love of freedom and the great outdoors.

CAPRICORN
Capricorns will be fascinated and inspired by the great historical monuments of Moscow, the most powerful of all Russian cities.

AQUARIUS
Intrepid Aquarians will be enthralled and amazed by the unusual sights and spectacular landscapes of the Indian subcontinent.

PISCES
Water-loving Pisceans will be at their most relaxed and romantic by the sea, perhaps on a small and unspoiled Mediterranean island.

THE PYRAMIDS, EGYPT

GONDOLAS, VENICE

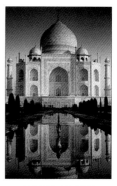

THE TAJ MAHAL, INDIA

VENUS & MARS

LUCID, SHINING VENUS AND FIERY, RED MARS HAVE ALWAYS BEEN
ASSOCIATED WITH HUMAN LOVE AND PASSION. THE TWO
PLANETS HAVE A POWERFUL INFLUENCE ON OUR ATTITUDES
TOWARD LOVE, SEX, AND RELATIONSHIPS.

*T*he study of astrology
first began long before
humankind began to record
its own history. The earliest
astrological artifacts discovered,
scratches on bones recording the
phases of the Moon, date from
well before the invention of any
alphabet or writing system.

The planets Venus and Mars
have always been regarded as
having enormous significance
in astrology. This is evident from
the tentative attempts of early
astrologers to record the effects
of the two planets on humankind.
Hundreds of years later, the
positions of the planets were
carefully noted in personal
horoscopes. The earliest known
record is dated 410 BC: "Venus
[was] in the Bull, and Mars in
the Twins."

The bright, shining planet Venus
represents the gentle effect of
the soul on our physical lives.
It is responsible for a refined
and romantic sensuality – "pure"
love, untainted by sex. Venus
reigns over our attitudes toward
romance and the spiritual
dimension of love.

The planet Mars affects the
physical aspects of our lives –
our strength, both physical
and mental; our endurance; and
our ability to fight for survival.
Mars is also strongly linked to
the sex drive of both men and
women. Mars governs our
physical energy, sexuality, and
levels of desire.

Venus is known as an
"inferior" planet, because its
orbit falls between Earth and
the Sun. Venus orbits the Sun

LOVE CONQUERS ALL

In Botticelli's Venus and Mars, *the warlike, fiery
energy of Mars, the god of war, has been overcome by
the gentle charms of Venus, the goddess of love.*

closely, and its position in the
zodiac is always in a sign near
that of the Sun. As a result, the
planet can only have occupied
one of five given signs at the
time of your birth – your Sun
sign, or the two signs before or
after it. For example, if you were
born with the Sun in Virgo,
Venus can only have occupied
Cancer, Leo, Virgo, Libra, or
Scorpio at that moment.

Mars, on the other hand, is
a "superior" planet. Its orbit lies
on the other side of Earth from

the Sun, and therefore the
planet may have occupied any
of the 12 signs at the moment
of your birth.

On the following pages
(24–45) we provide you with
fascinating insights into how
Mars and Venus govern your
attitudes toward love, sex, and
relationships. To ascertain which
sign of the zodiac the planets
occupied at the moment of
your birth, you must first consult
the tables on pages 52–61. Then
turn to page 24 and read on.

YOUR LOVE LIFE

THE PLANET VENUS REPRESENTS LOVE, HARMONY, AND UNITY.
WORK OUT WHICH SIGN OF THE ZODIAC VENUS OCCUPIED AT
THE MOMENT OF YOUR BIRTH (SEE PAGES 52–57), AND READ ON.

VENUS IN SCORPIO

*C*apricornians make witty, reliable, and supportive lovers, but with this placing your attitude toward romance will be transformed by Scorpio's passion and intensity. The rather cool and undemonstrative manner typical of many Capricorns is likely to be replaced by a more emotional and responsive manner.

Although Venus in Scorpio will underline your need for a harmonious and rewarding relationship, you may have some difficulty in finding a suitable partner. Capricorn is a careful and prudent sign, and you will not want to make an emotional investment until you are sure it will result in a happy, long-lasting relationship. Venus in Scorpio may push you to make a

commitment, but Capricorn will sound a note of caution and hold you back, even if every other instinct urges you to throw yourself into a relationship.

Due to the intensity and fervor of Scorpio, you will take your affairs of the heart very seriously. Do not fall into the trap of becoming overprotective or obsessive about your alliance, because you may create a restrictive atmosphere, which will alarm your partner. Luckily, the dry Capricorn sense of humor should help you to retain your sense of perspective.

Capricorn is a controlled and disciplined sign, and you will mistrust overt displays of emotion. However, you must not repress the passion and power of

Scorpio emotions. The intensity of Venus in Scorpio will temper your Capricorn coolness and reserve, adding greatly to your powers of attraction.

With this planetary placing, Scorpio jealousy may manifest itself. If this unpleasant quality manages to gain a foothold in your personality, you may become moody and suspicious of your partner. Beware of becoming too possessive, or of making rash accusations. If your jealousy gets out of control, your lover might not be able to tolerate it, and the green-eyed monster may drive you both apart.

If you are able to combine the practicality, discipline, and humor of Capricorn with the abundant passion and emotion that Venus brings from Scorpio, you will be an inspiring, caring, and devoted lover, with plenty of potential partners.

VENUS IN SAGITTARIUS

*W*hen Venus shines from Sagittarius, you will be far more approachable and amiable than many of your fellow Capricorns. You will possess a great capacity for enjoyment and socializing, and will be able to express your feelings in an affectionate, warm, and honest fashion.

Due to the influence of Sagittarius, you will treasure your independence, and consequently you may be cautious about committing yourself to a long-term relationship. You will think very carefully about the effect a permanent alliance will have on your life, and will weigh all the advantages and disadvantages at great length.

When a Capricorn decides that it is time to form a long-term relationship, a potential partner may be selected for the wrong reasons, such as extreme physical attractiveness,

wealth, or power. Fortunately, when Venus shines from Sagittarius, you are much less likely to be influenced by material considerations, and more ready to be attracted by cheerfulness and intelligence. This is an entirely beneficial addition to your personality. If you are to remain constant and faithful to your lover for life, a strong element of friendship and intellectual rapport must provide the foundation of your relationship.

The loyalty and faithfulness of Capricorn may be undermined by the influence of carefree, irresponsible Sagittarius. Boredom strikes fear into your heart, and you cannot tolerate monotony. The serious-minded nature of Capricorn will be lightened by this placing, and you will be a seeker of novelty, entertainment, and fun. If you are bored, you may become dissatisfied and

restless, and will begin to look around for thrills and excitement. The duality of Sagittarius may even encourage you to seek excitement in the form of illicit affairs. Such behavior is utterly atypical of Capricorn, which is usually an extremely faithful and constant sign. Fortunately, you are very practical and forward-thinking, and will take the complications of any clandestine liaisons in your stride.

You are an outgoing and good-natured friend, and will raise the spirits of all around you. Capricorn usually dislikes noise and excitement, but Sagittarius revels in a little drama, and you will be an ebullient companion. The optimism of blithe and breezy Sagittarius will vanquish the determined pessimism of Capricorn, and consequently you will be an encouraging, lively, and supportive partner.

VENUS IN CAPRICORN

*W*hen Venus and the Sun both shine from Capricorn, you will take your romantic relationships very seriously. Capricorn tends to be extremely cautious about commitment, and consequently you are not likely to rush into a relationship in a hurry. You will make sure that you know your lover well before you become seriously involved. Cautious and intensely practical, you will not want to invest your emotions in a relationship unless you are confident that it will be a success.

Due to this placing, once you make a commitment, you will be a constant and reliable lover. However, you are not likely to make gushing and sentimental declarations of love to your partner, and will not treat him or her to any overt displays of affection. You are not naturally demonstrative, and may find discussing your emotions somewhat embarrassing. You must remember to reassure your partner of your love frequently; your lover may interpret your Capricorn coolness and self-control as a lack of interest or desire on your part.

This planetary placing will underline all your Capricorn traits. Material status and wealth will be particularly important to you, because they represent emotional security, stability, and success. There is a danger that you may choose a partner for the wrong reasons – because he or she is particularly attractive, affluent, or influential, and is therefore a status symbol in his or her own right.

With such a "trophy" on your arm, you may feel that you are enhancing your image and exciting envy among your friends and aquaintances. You must not choose a lifelong partner just to boost your ego.

Instead, look for a lover who will encourage you to meet your ambitions, and who will remain a faithful and honest soul mate through good times and bad.

Once settled in a permanent relationship, you will want to be a good provider, and will work hard to make plenty of money to support your lover. Do not go to extremes and devote all your time to your work, or you may begin to neglect your partner.

Due to the double influence of Capricorn, you can appear proud and reserved. You are concerned with keeping up appearances, and possess a dignified and self-possessed demeanor. Make sure that you do not inadvertently give the impression of being snobbish and unfriendly. This could not be farther from the truth, for beneath your cool exterior is a fond, reliable, and supportive friend and lover.

VENUS IN AQUARIUS

*I*rresistibly attractive, with an aloof air of glamor, a Capricorn with Venus in Aquarius will not suffer from a shortage of potential partners. However, due to the fierce independence of Aquarius and the caution of Capricorn, you may distance yourself from your admirers, and will be in no hurry to find a partner and settle down.

You enjoy attention and admiration, and will accept it graciously, but when it becomes obvious that an admirer is very eager to enter into a long-term relationship, you are likely to back off swiftly. You will cling to your solitude and guard your independence jealously.

When it comes to choosing a lover, Capricorns tend to be extremely fussy and difficult to please, especially if they are contemplating a permanent relationship. This quality will be enhanced by Venus in

Aquarius. You may feel that no one can quite measure up to your high standards. However, your fastidiousness could be just an excuse to delay commitment.

When you do begin to woo someone seriously, you may discover previously unsuspected depths of romance in your personality. However, you may find it difficult to express your emotions. This is often a problem for restrained Capricorns, and Venus in Aquarius will not be able to offer you a great deal of help. You may feel wary when it comes to showing your feelings, and you will regard any soul baring as self-indulgent and embarassing. Try to overcome this mental block – it is possible to articulate your feelings in a cool and rational manner.

The steady and sensible influence of Capricorn will be diluted by the unpredictable eccentricity of Aquarius, perhaps

the most idiosyncratic of all the signs. You will be witty and unconventional – both appealing characteristics. However, you may not possess an abundance of warmth or affection. When you become involved, train yourself to be more demonstrative toward your partner, or he or she may feel insecure and unloved.

Although you appear rather impersonal, you are kind and sociable, and make a loyal and supportive friend. You are always ready to give helpful advice to anyone in need, and therefore will be very popular.

When you do commit yourself, you will be a faithful and supportive partner. Venus in Aquarius will make you a true romantic at heart, and you must not suppress this delightful quality, because it is particularly appealing and attractive to a prospective lover.

VENUS IN PISCES

*T*his placing will warm your cool Capricornian heart, and your emotional level will be greatly increased. Indeed, a powerful flood of emotion will sweep over you, washing away any Capricorn inhibitions. Consequently, your attitude toward your lover will be tender, passionate, and affectionate.

The influence of Pisces will make you a great romantic, and you may fall in love with the very notion of being in love. This tendency could make you too hasty when choosing a lover, and you may make a mistake in your choice of partner. Only experience will teach you to be more careful with your gift of love. However, as a Sun-sign Capricorn you should have plenty of common sense to draw upon when selecting a lover.

When Venus shines from Pisces, you will possess a huge capacity for selfless love and adoration. You will lavish all your time and attention on your partner, but must make sure that he or she does not take advantage of your love and support. Do not allow your partner to turn you into a doormat and exploit your good nature. You are extremely trusting, even gullible, and this belief in others may lead to hurt and disillusionment if your lover or friends let you down. Although the increased emotion brought by Pisces will benefit you greatly, do not allow it to overpower your good sense. Instead, utilize all the prudence and caution of Capricorn, and you should be both loving and sensitive, yet sensible and practical.

Due to the influence of Pisces, you will have a strong need to express your feelings openly, which is not easy for reserved Capricorns. However, Pisces will easily overpower the introverted nature of Capricorn,

and you may even tend toward sentimentality, which will make it much easier for you to make declarations of love.

There is a danger that an element of self-deception could reveal itself in your character. You may deal with problems by simply ignoring their existence. However, sensible Capricorn should help you face up to any difficulties, and sort them out in a rational, coolheaded fashion.

Capricorn does not generally suffer from a lack of confidence, but when you are attracted to someone, you may be reluctant to make an approach, doubting your powers of attraction. This self-doubt is one of the less beneficial effects of Venus in Pisces. Do not denigrate yourself, because you are a warm, tender partner, combining elements of gentle romanticism and prudent practicality in your character.

YOUR SEX LIFE

THE PLANET MARS REPRESENTS PHYSICAL AND SEXUAL ENERGY.
WORK OUT WHICH SIGN OF THE ZODIAC MARS OCCUPIED AT THE
MOMENT OF YOUR BIRTH (SEE PAGES 58–61), AND READ ON.

MARS IN ARIES

From Aries, Mars will bring you a particularly high level of physical energy and may provide a welcome boost to your sexual drive. Capricorns can appear somewhat chilly and undemonstrative, but those born with Mars in Aries will make much more passionate, warm-hearted, and energetic lovers.

Capricorn caution will be vanquished by the impetuosity that Mars brings from Aries; when attracted to someone you will make your interest clear. Your honesty and optimism are appealing, and your lovemaking will be ardent and enthusiastic, untainted by the cool restraint so typical of Capricorn.

MARS IN TAURUS

When Mars is in Taurus, you will possess a strong and powerful sexual appetite. An injection of Taurean sensuality will greatly benefit your sex life, and you are likely to be an ardent, dynamic, and yet tender lover.

There is a possibility that Mars may bring you an element of Taurean possessiveness. Do not become overprotective of your lover. A claustrophobic atmosphere may pervade your relationship, and your lover may feel confined by your love.

Capricorn is an unemotional and controlled sign, but from Taurus, Mars may bring you a hot temper. When your anger is roused, you can fly into a rage. Your lover may be intimidated by your fury; therefore, allow cool Capricorn to calm your emotions.

The adventurousness of Mars can be subdued by Taurus, but don't allow yourself to get stuck in a rut. You possess plenty of energy and imagination, so try to be inventive when it comes to exploring your sexuality.

MARS IN GEMINI

*C*apricornians tend to be extremely conventional and conformist, but when Mars shines from Gemini you will adopt a far more lighthearted and adventurous attitude toward your sexuality. Your lover will be thrilled by your imaginative and inventive lovemaking.

The steadiness and stolidity of earthy Capricorn will be lightened by the restless and frivolous influence of vivacious Gemini. You are likely to possess a hint of Geminian duality,

and as a result the prospect of illicit affairs may excite you. This is a far cry from the usual constancy and faithfulness of loyal Capricorn.

The lighthearted, sparkling influence of Gemini will make you lively and carefree, and any Capricorn pessimism should be dispelled by this placing. Although Capricorn is a very diligent and hardworking sign, Gemini should make you more sociable and gregarious, and you will both work and play hard.

MARS IN CANCER

*T*he gentle and emotional influence of Mars in Cancer will transform you into a sensitive, considerate, and tender lover. From this sign, Mars will greatly increase your passion and sensuality, and an active, satisfying sex life will be most important to you.

Mars in Cancer will make you treasure your domestic life above all else, and you will be motivated by a very powerful desire to find a partner and settle down. This deep yearning for a secure emotional relationship should overcome any Capricorn caution about making a long-term commitment.

From Cancer, Mars may bring you a tendency toward over-sensitivity. Consequently, you may interpret the most innocent comments as harsh criticisms, and then retreat into a sulk. Try not to hold onto your resentment. Instead, make use of the good sense and dry humor of Capricorn – these qualities will help you to forgive and forget.

MARS IN LEO

*T*his placing of Mars will add warmth, optimism, and enthusiasm to your prudent Capricorn personality. Mars in Leo will also heighten your sexuality, making you a dynamic and sensual lover. Consequently, your lovemaking will be ardent, passionate, and rewarding.

The generous influence of Leo will make you an extremely considerate and solicitous lover. However, once you are happily settled in a long-term relationship, practical Capricorn may assert itself, and you may feel that it is unnecessary to lavish quite so much time and money on your lover. Make sure that you do not begin to neglect your partner and your domestic life, and avoid concentrating all your efforts on the advancement of your career.

You may be prone to sudden explosions of temper. These may be intimidating, but fortunately your rage will die down as quickly as it flares up, and any unexpected storms will soon blow over and be forgotten.

MARS IN VIRGO

The modest and diffident influence of Mars in Virgo will not be able to add much warmth or passion to your cool Capricorn personality. However, both Capricorn and Virgo are earth signs, and if your lover can break through your dignified and formal exterior, he or she will discover that you are an ardent and sensual lover.

Capricorns are extremely cautious about making a long-term commitment, and the influence of Virgo is likely to make you extremely fastidious. You will have to look very long and hard before you find a lover who comes up to your high standards. Try not to become too fussy and discriminating.

Both Virgo and Capricorn are extremely conscientious and diligent signs; therefore, you may find it difficult to tear yourself away from your work. Once you have found a lover and settled down, you must not neglect him or her by devoting all your time to your career.

MARS IN LIBRA

From romantic Libra, the powerful influence of Mars may overcome the caution and prudence of Capricorn, and persuade you to fall in love at first sight. Although Mars will not be able to boost your energy from this sign, it will enhance your sensuality, and you will be a responsive and exciting lover.

In order to keep you content, a relationship must offer you love, security, and a fulfilling sex life. However, you are likely to have the usual Capricorn devotion to your career. If your work usurps too much of your time and energy, you will be torn between devoting your time to your job and your relationship.

You are generally an enthusiastic lover, but your partner will never quite know what sexual response to expect from you. Sometimes you will demand a strenous night of passion, but at other times you are just as likely to want to curl up in bed with your cat and a good book.

MARS IN SCORPIO

*M*ars in Scorpio is a passionate and powerful placing, and the detachment and self-possession of Capricorn will be infused with a strong sexual undercurrent from Scorpio. The cool and unapproachable air of Capricorn will become tantalizing and alluring, and you will be an energetic and seductive lover with a remarkably high sex drive.

The passion of Scorpio is intensified by the sexual energy of Mars. Anyone born with this placing must find rewarding and fulfilling sexual expression. If you do not achieve total sexual fulfillment, you are likely to experience a feeling of inexplicable dissatisfaction.

This planetary placing may make you vulnerable to strong feelings of possessiveness and jealousy. You must recognize this unattractive tendency in yourself, and firmly control any irrational surges of jealousy, because your lover may be alarmed by your domineering attitude and the brooding intensity of your love.

- YOUR SEX LIFE -

MARS IN SAGITTARIUS

*M*ars in Sagittarius will bring you a great deal of sexual and intellectual energy, and you will need a responsive partner who can match your ardor and dynamism in the bedroom. As a lover, you are athletic and adventurous, and your lovemaking will always be exciting and energetic.

Due to the influence of Mars from Sagittarius, you will treasure your independence and freedom, and may be reluctant to make a long-term commitment.

When you do decide that it is time to settle down, your Capricorn caution will make you extremely cautious and discriminating, and your search for a lover may take some time.

When you have settled down in a permanent relationship, the restless influence of Mars in Sagittarius may encourage you to become involved in illicit affairs. However, infidelity is generally unusual in a Capricorn, because faithfulness and loyalty are very important to you.

MARS IN CAPRICORN

*W*hen Mars shines from Capricorn, your tenacity and diligence will be doubled. You will be determined to excel at all you become involved in, including your emotional relationships. You will put a lot of effort into lovemaking, and will be a skillful, sensual lover.

When you are attracted to someone, you will purposefully set out to win him or her over. Any competition from other admirers will only increase your persistence and determination.

You will not rest until you have won your lover's heart and settled down together in domestic bliss. The notion of infidelity will not appeal, and consequently you will be a constant and loyal partner.

Capricorns will work hard to be successful in their careers and their relationships. However, you must beware of devoting too much of your time and energy to your work. Your lover may begin to feel neglected and resentful, and could even seek attention from someone else.

MARS IN AQUARIUS

*A*ll Capricornians are naturally cautious about entering into a long-term relationship. When Mars is in Aquarius the influence of the sign will increase that caution considerably. You will be very fastidious in your choice of lover, and will not be happy with a jealous or possessive partner.

Mars in Aquarius is also likely to increase your cool and detached nature, and potential lovers may find it difficult to get close to you. You treasure your independence, and tend to shrink away from intimacy. However, once you take the plunge and settle down with a partner, you will be an extremely uninhibited and exciting lover.

Capricorns are deeply conventional, but this placing will bring a dash of Aquarian nonconformity, and you may have an eccentric streak. Do not become too outrageous – you are conventional by nature, and highly unorthodox behavior will worry your friends and lovers.

MARS IN PISCES

This placing will make you emotional, responsive, and sensitive, and you will be an extremely tender and seductive lover. You will possess a colorful imagination, and your lovemaking will be adventurous and inventive.

Although Capricorns tend to possess rather dignified and formal exteriors, Mars in Pisces will instill a positive desire in you to show warmth and affection – a very attractive quality that should be a considerable help to you in your search for a partner.

Try not to allow the practicality of Capricorn to dampen the charming romance and idealism of Pisces. You must encourage your daydreams and your starry-eyed romanticism, because these qualities will easily vanquish the pessimism and cynicism of Capricorn.

Mars in Pisces can be rather overemotional, and you may be a little too sensitive, but the irrepressible Capricorn sense of humor should help you to retain your perspective.

TOKENS OF LOVE

ASTROLOGY CAN GIVE YOU A FASCINATING INSIGHT INTO YOUR
LOVER'S PERSONALITY AND ATTITUDE TOWARD LOVE. IT CAN
ALSO PROVIDE YOU WITH SOME INVALUABLE HINTS WHEN YOU
WANT TO CHOOSE THE PERFECT GIFT FOR YOUR LOVER.

JEWELED
HAIR CLIP

ARIES
*The head is the part of the
body ruled by Aries, and
unusual hair accessories
will be greatly appreciated.*

DECORATIVE
COMB

LIMOGES
PORCELAIN
PILLBOX

TAURUS
*Taureans always
value quality above
quantity. Fine hand-
painted porcelain
is sure to appeal,
as will a plump,
luxurious cushion.*

TAPESTRY
CUSHION

SILVER CHARM
BRACELET

GEMINI
*Geminians love pieces
of jewelry, particularly
rings and bracelets.*

- TOKENS OF LOVE -

CANCER

A dainty sunshade will help to protect the delicate Cancerian skin. Pearl is the Cancerian gemstone and will be greatly cherished.

NATURAL
FRESHWATER
PEARLS

HAND-
PAINTED
CHINESE
SUNSHADE

GOLD
"COCKTAIL"
WRISTWATCH

LEO

Gold is the Leo metal; therefore, anything gold or gold-colored is guaranteed to delight your Leo lover.

GARDENING
TOOLS

REGENCY-
STYLE CHAIR

VIRGO

Virgo, an earth sign, naturally loves toiling in the soil. Any gardening implements will therefore be gratefully received, as well as any objects made from wood.

– TOKENS OF LOVE –

LIBRA
*Librans will enjoy
a recording of their
favorite classical music.
They revel in luxury,
and will be captivated
by seductive lingerie*

VIOLIN

SILKY
FRENCH
LINGERIE

DECORATIVE
TOOTHBRUSH

SCORPIO
*Decorative bathroom
accessories are sure
to appeal to your
Scorpio lover
because Scorpio
is a water sign.*

ENAMELED
GLOBE PILLBOX

SAGITTARIUS
*Adventurous
Sagittarians love
to travel; therefore,
any travel-related
gifts will be a
great success.*

VICTORIAN
TRAVEL BOOKS

LINEN POCKET
HANDKERCHIEFS

CAPRICORN

*Pure linen handkerchiefs
will delight a fastidious
Capricorn lover.*

AQUARIUS

*Aquarians
adore unusual
and original gifts.
Handmade
modern pottery
and glass will
enchant your
Aquarian lover.*

GIVING A BIRTHSTONE

*The most personal
gift you can give
your lover is the
gem linked to his
or her Sun sign.*

AMETHYST

ARIES: *diamond*
TAURUS: *emerald*
GEMINI: *agate* · CANCER: *pearl*
LEO: *ruby* · VIRGO: *sardonyx*
LIBRA: *sapphire* · SCORPIO: *opal*
SAGITTARIUS: *topaz*
CAPRICORN: *amethyst*
AQUARIUS: *aquamarine*
PISCES: *moonstone*

HAND-BLOWN
GLASS GOBLET

IRIDESCENT
GLASS
MARBLES

DECORATIVE
SHELL

PISCES

*Pisces is a water sign;
therefore, a Piscean
will be captivated by
a decorative shell.
Iridescent glassware
is also guaranteed
to please.*

YOUR PERMANENT RELATIONSHIP

CAPRICORNS APPROACH A PERMANENT RELATIONSHIP
WITH SOME CAUTION. HOWEVER, ONCE COMMITTED, THEY ARE
AMONG THE MOST LOYAL AND FAITHFUL LOVERS.

*O*nce they enter into a long-term relationship, Capricorns will work very hard at it. However, you are naturally cautious, and will only enter into a relationship after having made certain in your own mind that you are doing the right thing. Having decided to become involved, you will take your partnership very seriously, and make a constant, faithful, and steady lover.

You look for quality in every area of your life, and will certainly look for it in your partners. They will have be smart, good-looking, and socially adept, as well as able to cope with any situation, whether social or emotional – in short, a real paragon of virtue.

One less attractive Capricorn trait is a tendency toward social climbing and snobbishness. It is not unknown for Capricorn to choose a partner for the enhanced social status or increased career prospects he or she may bring. Such considerations are not sound reasons for an alliance, and they will not bring lasting happiness.

Your eagerness for your alliance to succeed may create the biggest problem in your relationship. There is a danger that you may work too hard for your family, and instead of spending time with them you may spend it working for them. If you have to choose between a weekend at home with your partner, or a weekend at a

A JOINT FUTURE
On a Sailing Ship, *by Caspar David Friedrich, shows a newly married couple sailing into a bright but unknown future together.*

business seminar, try not to automatically choose the work option. Guard against this tendency by making sure that you devote some time every day to your family. If your great qualities of drive and motivation are used wisely, they can prove a very positive attributes, leading to a rewarding lifestyle.

If conflicts occur, remember the importance of talking all your problems through with your partner. Capricorns do not always find discussion easy, and tend to dislike opening up to anyone, even their partner.

Try to overcome your natural reticence, and force yourself to be open with your lover.

Your dry sense of humor is particularly attractive, and if you share your appreciation of the lighter side of life, it will greatly benefit your relationship.

VENUS & MARS TABLES

THESE TABLES WILL ENABLE YOU TO DISCOVER WHICH SIGNS
VENUS AND MARS OCCUPIED AT THE MOMENT OF YOUR BIRTH.
TURN TO PAGES 24–45 TO INVESTIGATE THE QUALITIES OF THESE
SIGNS, AND TO FIND OUT HOW THEY WORK WITH YOUR SUN SIGN.

*T*he tables on pages 53–61 will enable you to discover the positions of Venus and Mars at the moment of your birth.

First find your year of birth on the top line of the appropriate table, then find your month of birth in the left-hand column. Where the column for your year of birth intersects with the row for your month of birth, you will find a group of figures and zodiacal glyphs. These figures and glyphs show which sign of the zodiac the planet occupied

on the first day of that month, and any date during that month on which the planet moved into another sign.

For example, to ascertain the position of Venus on May 10, 1968, run your finger down the column marked 1968 until you reach the row for May. The row of numbers and glyphs shows that Venus occupied Aries on May 1, entered Taurus on May 4, and then moved into Gemini on May 28. Therefore, on May 10, Venus was in Taurus.

If you were born on a day when one of the planets was moving into a new sign, it may be impossible to determine your Venus and Mars signs completely accurately. If the characteristics described on the relevant pages do not seem to apply to you, read the interpretation of the sign before and after. One of these signs will be appropriate.

ZODIACAL GLYPHS

♈	Aries	♎	Libra
♉	Taurus	♏	Scorpio
♊	Gemini	♐	Sagittarius
♋	Cancer	♑	Capricorn
♌	Leo	♒	Aquarius
♍	Virgo	♓	Pisces

– VENUS TABLES –

♀	1921	1922	1923	1924	1925	1926	1927	1928
JAN	1 7 ♒ ♓	1 25 ♑ ♒	1 10 ♏ ♐	1 20 ♒ ♓	1 15 ♐ ♑	1 ♒	1 10 ♑ ♒	1 5 30 ♏ ♐ ♑
FEB	1 3 ♓ ♈	1 18 ♒ ♓	1 7 ♐ ♑	1 14 ♓ ♈	1 8 ♑ ♒	1 ♒	1 3 27 ♒ ♓ ♈	1 23 ♑ ♒
MAR	1 8 ♈ ♉	1 14 ♓ ♈	1 7 ♑ ♒	1 10 ♈ ♉	1 5 29 ♒ ♓ ♈	1 ♒	1 22 ♈ ♉	1 19 ♒ ♓
APR	1 26 ♉ ♈	1 7 ♈ ♉	1 2 27 ♒ ♓ ♈	1 6 ♉ ♊	1 22 ♈ ♉	1 7 ♒ ♓	1 17 ♉ ♊	1 12 ♓ ♈
MAY	1 ♈	1 2 26 ♉ ♊ ♋	1 22 ♈ ♉	1 7 ♊ ♋	1 16 ♉ ♊	1 7 ♓ ♈	1 13 ♊ ♋	1 7 31 ♈ ♉ ♊
JUN	1 3 ♈ ♉	1 20 ♋ ♌	1 16 ♉ ♊	1 ♋	1 10 ♊ ♋	1 3 29 ♈ ♉ ♊	1 9 ♋ ♌	1 24 ♊ ♋
JUL	1 9 ♉ ♊	1 16 ♌ ♍	1 11 ♊ ♋	1 ♋	1 4 29 ♋ ♌ ♍	1 25 ♊ ♋	1 8 ♌ ♍	1 19 ♋ ♌
AUG	1 6 ♊ ♋	1 11 ♍ ♎	1 4 28 ♋ ♌ ♍	1 ♋	1 23 ♍ ♎	1 19 ♋ ♌	1 ♍	1 12 ♌ ♍
SEP	1 27 ♌ ♍	1 8 ♎ ♏	1 22 ♍ ♎	1 8 ♋ ♌	1 17 ♎ ♏	1 12 ♌ ♍	1 ♍	1 5 30 ♍ ♎ ♏
OCT	1 21 ♍ ♎	1 11 ♏ ♐	1 16 ♎ ♏	1 ♌ ♍	1 12 ♏ ♐	1 6 30 ♍ ♎ ♏	1 ♍	1 24 ♏ ♐
NOV	1 14 ♎ ♏	1 29 ♐ ♏	1 9 ♏ ♐	1 3 28 ♍ ♎ ♏	1 7 ♐ ♑	1 23 ♏ ♐	1 10 ♍ ♎	1 18 ♐ ♑
DEC	1 8 31 ♏ ♐ ♑	1 ♏	1 3 27 ♐ ♑ ♒	1 22 ♏ ♐	1 6 ♑ ♒	1 ♐	1 9 ♎ ♏	1 13 ♑ ♒

♀	1929	1930	1931	1932	1933	1934	1935	1936
JAN	1 7 ♒ ♓	1 25 ♑ ♒	1 4 ♏ ♐	1 20 ♒ ♓	1 15 ♐ ♑	1 ♒	1 9 ♑ ♒	1 4 29 ♏ ♐ ♑
FEB	1 3 ♓ ♈	1 17 ♒ ♓	1 7 ♐ ♑	1 13 ♓ ♈	1 8 ♑ ♒	1 ♒	1 2 27 ♒ ♓ ♈	1 23 ♑ ♒
MAR	1 9 ♈ ♉	1 13 ♓ ♈	1 6 ♑ ♒	1 10 ♈ ♉	1 4 28 ♒ ♓ ♈	1 ♒	1 23 ♈ ♉	1 18 ♒ ♓
APR	1 21 ♉ ♈	1 7 ♈ ♉	1 2 27 ♒ ♓ ♈	1 6 ♉ ♊	1 21 ♈ ♉	1 7 ♒ ♓	1 17 ♉ ♊	1 12 ♓ ♈
MAY	1 ♈	1 2 26 ♉ ♊ ♋	1 22 ♈ ♉	1 7 ♊ ♋	1 16 ♉ ♊	1 7 ♓ ♈	1 12 ♊ ♋	1 6 30 ♈ ♉ ♊
JUN	1 4 ♈ ♉	1 20 ♋ ♌	1 15 ♉ ♊	1 ♋	1 9 ♊ ♋	1 3 29 ♈ ♉ ♊	1 8 ♋ ♌	1 24 ♊ ♋
JUL	1 9 ♉ ♊	1 15 ♌ ♍	1 10 ♊ ♋	1 14 29 ♋ ♊ ♋	1 4 28 ♋ ♌ ♍	1 24 ♊ ♋	1 8 ♌ ♍	1 18 ♋ ♌
AUG	1 6 ♊ ♋	1 11 ♍ ♎	1 4 28 ♋ ♌ ♍	1 ♋	1 22 ♍ ♎	1 18 ♋ ♌	1 ♍	1 12 ♌ ♍
SEP	1 26 ♌ ♍	1 8 ♎ ♏	1 21 ♍ ♎	1 9 ♋ ♌	1 16 ♎ ♏	1 12 ♌ ♍	1 ♍	1 5 29 ♍ ♎ ♏
OCT	1 21 ♍ ♎	1 13 ♏ ♐	1 15 ♎ ♏	1 8 ♌ ♍	1 12 ♏ ♐	1 6 30 ♍ ♎ ♏	1 ♍	1 24 ♏ ♐
NOV	1 14 ♎ ♏	1 23 ♐ ♏	1 8 ♏ ♐	1 3 28 ♍ ♎ ♏	1 7 ♐ ♑	1 23 ♏ ♐	1 10 ♍ ♎	1 17 ♐ ♑
DEC	1 8 31 ♏ ♐ ♑	1 ♏	1 2 26 ♐ ♑ ♒	1 22 ♏ ♐	1 6 ♑ ♒	1 ♐	1 17 ♎ ♏	1 12 ♑ ♒

♀	1937	1938	1939	1940	1941	1942	1943	1944
JAN	1 ♒ · 7 ♓	1 ♑ · 24 ♒	1 ♏ · 5 ♐	1 ♒ · 19 ♓	1 ♐ · 14 ♑	1 ♒	1 ♑ · 9 ♒	1 ♏ · 4 ♐ · 29 ♑
FEB	1 ♓ · 3 ♈	1 ♒ · 17 ♓	1 ♐ · 7 ♑	1 ♓ · 13 ♈	1 ♑ · 7 ♒	1 ♒	1 ♒ · 2 ♓ · 26 ♈	1 ♑ · 22 ♒
MAR	1 ♈ · 10 ♉	1 ♓ · 13 ♈	1 ♑ · 6 ♒	1 ♈ · 9 ♉	1 ♒ · 3 ♓ · 28 ♈	1 ♒	1 ♈ · 22 ♉	1 ♒ · 18 ♓
APR	1 ♉ · 15 ♈	1 ♈ · 6 ♉ · 30 ♊	1 ♓ · 26 ♈	1 ♉ · 5 ♊	1 ♈ · 21 ♉	1 ♒ · 7 ♓	1 ♉ · 16 ♈	1 ♓ · 11 ♈
MAY	1 ♈	1 ♊ · 25 ♋	1 ♈ · 21 ♉	1 ♊ · 7 ♋	1 ♉ · 15 ♊	1 ♓ · 7 ♈	1 ♈ · 12 ♉	1 ♈ · 5 ♉ · 30 ♊
JUN	1 ♈ · 5 ♉	1 ♋ · 19 ♌	1 ♉ · 15 ♊	1 ♋	1 ♊ · 8 ♋	1 ♈ · 3 ♉ · 28 ♊	1 ♉ · 8 ♊	1 ♊ · 23 ♋
JUL	1 ♉ · 8 ♊	1 ♌ · 15 ♍	1 ♊ · 10 ♋	1 ♋ · 6 ♊	1 ♋ · 3 ♌ · 28 ♍	1 ♊ · 24 ♋	1 ♊ · 8 ♋	1 ♋ · 18 ♌
AUG	1 ♊ · 4 ♋	1 ♍ · 10 ♎	1 ♋ · 3 ♌ · 27 ♍	1 ♊ · 2 ♋	1 ♍ · 22 ♎	1 ♋ · 18 ♌	1 ♋ · 18 ♌	1 ♌ · 11 ♍
SEP	1 ♌ · 26 ♍	1 ♎ · 8 ♏	1 ♍ · 21 ♎	1 ♋ · 9 ♌	1 ♎ · 16 ♏	1 ♌ · 11 ♍	1 ♌ · 11 ♍	1 ♍ · 4 ♎ · 29 ♏
OCT	1 ♍ · 20 ♎	1 ♏ · 14 ♐	1 ♎ · 15 ♏	1 ♌ · 11 ♍	1 ♏ · 11 ♐	1 ♍ · 5 ♎ · 29 ♏	1 ♍	1 ♏ · 23 ♐
NOV	1 ♎ · 13 ♏	1 ♐ · 16 ♏	1 ♏ · 8 ♐	1 ♍ · 2 ♎ · 27 ♏	1 ♐ · 7 ♑	1 ♏ · 22 ♐	1 ♎ · 10 ♏	1 ♐ · 17 ♑
DEC	1 ♏ · 7 ♐ · 31 ♑	1 ♏	1 ♐ · 2 ♑ · 26 ♒	1 ♏ · 21 ♐	1 ♑ · 6 ♒	1 ♐ · 16 ♑	1 ♎ · 9 ♏	1 ♑ · 12 ♒

♀	1945	1946	1947	1948	1949	1950	1951	1952
JAN	1 ♒ · 6 ♓	1 ♑ · 23 ♒	1 ♏ · 6 ♐	1 ♒ · 19 ♓	1 ♐ · 14 ♑	1 ♒	1 ♑ · 8 ♒	1 ♏ · 3 ♐ · 28 ♑
FEB	1 ♓ · 3 ♈	1 ♒ · 16 ♓	1 ♐ · 7 ♑	1 ♓ · 12 ♈	1 ♑ · 7 ♒	1 ♒	1 ♓ · 25 ♈	1 ♑ · 21 ♒
MAR	1 ♈ · 12 ♉	1 ♓ · 12 ♈	1 ♑ · 6 ♒	1 ♈ · 9 ♉	1 ♒ · 3 ♓ · 27 ♈	1 ♒	1 ♈ · 22 ♉	1 ♒ · 17 ♓
APR	1 ♉ · 8 ♈	1 ♈ · 6 ♉ · 30 ♊	1 ♓ · 26 ♈	1 ♉ · 5 ♊	1 ♈ · 20 ♉	1 ♒ · 7 ♓	1 ♉ · 16 ♈	1 ♓ · 10 ♈
MAY	1 ♈	1 ♊ · 25 ♋	1 ♈ · 21 ♉	1 ♊ · 8 ♋	1 ♉ · 15 ♊	1 ♓ · 6 ♈	1 ♈ · 12 ♉	1 ♈ · 5 ♉ · 29 ♊
JUN	1 ♈ · 5 ♉	1 ♋ · 19 ♌	1 ♉ · 14 ♊	1 ♋ · 30 ♊	1 ♊ · 8 ♋	1 ♈ · 2 ♉ · 28 ♊	1 ♉ · 8 ♊	1 ♊ · 23 ♋
JUL	1 ♉ · 8 ♊	1 ♌ · 14 ♍	1 ♊ · 9 ♋	1 ♊	1 ♋ · 2 ♌ · 27 ♍	1 ♊ · 23 ♋	1 ♊ · 9 ♋	1 ♋ · 17 ♌
AUG	1 ♊ · 5 ♋ · 31 ♌	1 ♍ · 9 ♎	1 ♋ · 3 ♌ · 27 ♍	1 ♊ · 2 ♋	1 ♍ · 21 ♎	1 ♋ · 17 ♌	1 ♋ · 16 ♌	1 ♌ · 10 ♍
SEP	1 ♌ · 25 ♍	1 ♎ · 8 ♏	1 ♍ · 20 ♎	1 ♋ · 9 ♌	1 ♎ · 15 ♏	1 ♌ · 11 ♍	1 ♌ · 11 ♍	1 ♍ · 4 ♎ · 28 ♏
OCT	1 ♍ · 20 ♎	1 ♏ · 17 ♐	1 ♎ · 14 ♏	1 ♌ · 7 ♍	1 ♏ · 11 ♐	1 ♍ · 5 ♎ · 29 ♏	1 ♍	1 ♏ · 23 ♐
NOV	1 ♎ · 13 ♏	1 ♐ · 9 ♏	1 ♏ · 7 ♐	1 ♍ · 2 ♎ · 27 ♏	1 ♐ · 7 ♑	1 ♏ · 22 ♐	1 ♎ · 10 ♏	1 ♐ · 16 ♑
DEC	1 ♏ · 7 ♐ · 31 ♑	1 ♏	1 ♐ · 2 ♑ · 26 ♒	1 ♏ · 21 ♐	1 ♑ · 7 ♒	1 ♐ · 15 ♑	1 ♎ · 9 ♏	1 ♑ · 11 ♒

♀	1953	1954	1955	1956	1957	1958	1959	1960
JAN	1 ♒ 6 ♓	1 ♑ 23 ♒	1 ♏ 7 ♐	1 ♒ 18 ♓	1 ♐ 13 ♑	1 ♒	1 ♑ 8 ♒	1 ♏ 3 ♐ 28 ♑
FEB	1 ♓ 3 ♈	1 ♒ 16 ♓	1 ♐ 7 ♑	1 ♓ 12 ♈	1 ♑ 6 ♒	1 ♒	1 ♓ 25 ♈	1 ♑ 21 ♒
MAR	1 ♈ 15 ♉	1 ♓ 12 ♈	1 ♑ 5 ♒ 31 ♓	1 ♈ 8 ♉	1 ♒ 2 ♓ 26 ♈	1 ♒	1 ♈ 21 ♉	1 ♒ 16 ♓
APR	1 ♈	1 ♈ 5 ♉ 29 ♊	1 ♓ 25 ♈	1 ♉ 5 ♊	1 ♈ 19 ♉	1 ♒ 7 ♓	1 ♉ 15 ♊	1 ♓ 10 ♈
MAY	1 ♈	1 ♊ 24 ♋	1 ♈ 20 ♉	1 ♊ 9 ♋	1 ♉ 14 ♊	1 ♓ 6 ♈	1 ♊ 11 ♋	1 ♈ 4 ♉ 29 ♊
JUN	1 ♈ 6 ♉	1 ♋ 18 ♌	1 ♉ 14 ♊	1 ♋ 24 ♊	1 ♊ 7 ♋	1 ♈ 2 ♉ 27 ♊	1 ♋ 7 ♌	1 ♊ 22 ♋
JUL	1 ♉ 8 ♊	1 ♌ 14 ♍	1 ♊ 9 ♋	1 ♊	1 ♋ 2 ♌ 27 ♍	1 ♊ 22 ♋	1 ♌ 9 ♍	1 ♋ 16 ♌
AUG	1 ♊ 5 ♋ 31 ♌	1 ♍ 10 ♎	1 ♋ 5 ♌ 26 ♍	1 ♊ 5 ♋	1 ♍ 21 ♎	1 ♋ 16 ♌	1 ♍	1 ♌ 9 ♍
SEP	1 ♌ 25 ♍	1 ♎ 7 ♏	1 ♍ 19 ♎	1 ♋ 9 ♌	1 ♎ 15 ♏	1 ♌ 10 ♍	1 ♍ 21 ♌ 26 ♍	1 ♍ 3 ♎ 28 ♏
OCT	1 ♍ 19 ♎	1 ♏ 24 ♐ 28 ♏	1 ♎ 13 ♏	1 ♌ 7 ♍	1 ♏ 11 ♎	1 ♍ 3 ♎ 28 ♏	1 ♍	1 ♏ 22 ♐
NOV	1 ♎ 12 ♏	1 ♏	1 ♏ 6 ♐	1 ♎ 26 ♏	1 ♏ 6 ♐	1 ♏ 21 ♐	1 ♎ 10 ♏	1 ♐ 16 ♑
DEC	1 ♏ 6 ♐ 30 ♑	1 ♏	1 ♑ 25 ♒	1 ♏ 20 ♐	1 ♑ 7 ♒	1 ♐ 15 ♑	1 ♎ 8 ♏	1 ♑ 11 ♒

♀	1961	1962	1963	1964	1965	1966	1967	1968
JAN	1 ♒ 6 ♓	1 ♑ 22 ♒	1 ♏ 7 ♐	1 ♒ 17 ♓	1 ♐ 13 ♑	1 ♒	1 ♑ 7 ♒ 31 ♓	1 ♏ 2 ♐ 27 ♑
FEB	1 ♓ 3 ♈	1 ♒ 15 ♓	1 ♐ 6 ♑	1 ♓ 11 ♈	1 ♑ 6 ♒	1 ♒ 7 ♑ 26 ♒	1 ♓ 24 ♈	1 ♑ 21 ♒
MAR	1 ♈	1 ♓ 11 ♈	1 ♑ 5 ♒ 31 ♓	1 ♈ 8 ♉	1 ♒ 2 ♓ 26 ♈	1 ♒	1 ♈ 21 ♉	1 ♒ 16 ♓
APR	1 ♈	1 ♈ 4 ♉ 29 ♊	1 ♓ 25 ♈	1 ♉ 5 ♊	1 ♈ 19 ♉	1 ♒ 7 ♓	1 ♉ 15 ♊	1 ♓ 9 ♈
MAY	1 ♈	1 ♊ 24 ♋	1 ♈ 20 ♉	1 ♊ 10 ♋	1 ♉ 13 ♊	1 ♓ 6 ♈	1 ♊ 11 ♋	1 ♈ 4 ♉ 28 ♊
JUN	1 ♈ 6 ♉	1 ♋ 18 ♌	1 ♉ 13 ♊	1 ♋ 18 ♊	1 ♊ 7 ♋	1 ♉ 27 ♊	1 ♋ 7 ♌	1 ♊ 21 ♋
JUL	1 ♉ 8 ♊	1 ♌ 13 ♍	1 ♊ 8 ♋	1 ♊	1 ♋ 26 ♌	1 ♊ 22 ♋	1 ♌ 9 ♍	1 ♋ 16 ♌
AUG	1 ♊ 4 ♋ 30 ♌	1 ♍ 9 ♎	1 ♋ 26 ♌	1 ♊ 6 ♋	1 ♍ 20 ♎	1 ♋ 16 ♌	1 ♍	1 ♌ 9 ♍
SEP	1 ♌ 24 ♍	1 ♎ 8 ♏	1 ♍ 18 ♎	1 ♋ 9 ♌	1 ♎ 14 ♏	1 ♌ 9 ♍	1 ♍ 10 ♎	1 ♍ 3 ♎ 27 ♏
OCT	1 ♍ 18 ♎	1 ♏	1 ♎ 13 ♏	1 ♌ 6 ♍	1 ♏ 10 ♐	1 ♍ 3 ♎ 27 ♏	1 ♍ 2 ♎	1 ♏ 22 ♐
NOV	1 ♎ 12 ♏	1 ♏	1 ♏ 6 ♐ 30 ♑	1 ♎ 25 ♏	1 ♏ 6 ♐	1 ♏ 20 ♐	1 ♍ 10 ♎	1 ♐ 15 ♑
DEC	1 ♏ 6 ♐ 29 ♑	1 ♏	1 ♑ 24 ♒	1 ♏ 20 ♐	1 ♑ 8 ♒	1 ♐ 14 ♑	1 ♎ 8 ♏	1 ♑ 10 ♒

– VENUS TABLES –

♀	1969	1970	1971	1972	1973	1974	1975	1976
JAN	1 ♒ 5 ♓	1 ♑ 22 ♒	1 ♏ 8 ♐	1 ♒ 17 ♓	1 ♐ 12 ♑	1 ♒ 30 ♑	1 ♑ 7 ♒ 31 ♓	1 ♏ 7 ♐ 27 ♑
FEB	1 ♓ 3 ♈	1 ♒ 15 ♓	1 ♐ 6 ♑	1 ♓ 11 ♈	1 ♑ 5 ♒	1 ♑	1 ♓ 24 ♈	1 ♑ 20 ♒
MAR	1 ♈	1 ♓ 11 ♈	1 ♑ 5 ♒ 30 ♓	1 ♈ 25 ♉	1 ♓ 25 ♈	1 ♒	1 ♈ 20 ♉	1 ♒ 15 ♓
APR	1 ♈	1 ♈ 4 ♉ 28 ♊	1 ♓ 24 ♈	1 ♉ 4 ♊	1 ♈ 19 ♉	1 ♒ 7 ♓	1 ♉ 14 ♊	1 ♓ 9 ♈
MAY	1 ♈	1 ♊ 23 ♋	1 ♈ 19 ♉	1 ♊ 11 ♋	1 ♉ 13 ♊	1 ♓ 5 ♈	1 ♊ 10 ♋	1 ♈ 3 ♉ 27 ♊
JUN	1 ♈ 6 ♉	1 ♋ 17 ♌	1 ♉ 13 ♊	1 ♋ 12 ♊	1 ♊ 6 ♋	1 ♉ 26 ♊	1 ♋ 7 ♌	1 ♊ 21 ♋
JUL	1 ♉ 7 ♊	1 ♌ 13 ♍	1 ♊ 7 ♋	1 ♊	1 ♌ 26 ♍	1 ♊ 22 ♋	1 ♌ 10 ♍	1 ♋ 15 ♌
AUG	1 ♊ 4 ♋ 30 ♌	1 ♍ 9 ♎	1 ♌ 25 ♍	1 ♊ 7 ♋	1 ♍ 19 ♎	1 ♋ 15 ♌	1 ♍	1 ♌ 9 ♍
SEP	1 ♌ 24 ♍	1 ♎ 8 ♏	1 ♍ 18 ♎	1 ♋ 8 ♌	1 ♎ 14 ♏	1 ♌ 9 ♍	1 ♍ 3 ♌	1 ♍ 2 ♎ 26 ♏
OCT	1 ♍ 18 ♎	1 ♏	1 ♎ 12 ♏	1 ♌ 6 ♍ 31 ♎	1 ♏ 7 ♐	1 ♍ 3 ♎ 27 ♏	1 ♌ 21 ♍	1 ♏ 21 ♐
NOV	1 ♎ 11 ♏	1 ♏	1 ♏ 5 ♐ 30 ♑	1 ♎ 25 ♏	1 ♐ 6 ♑	1 ♏ 20 ♐	1 ♍ 10 ♎	1 ♐ 15 ♑
DEC	1 ♏ 5 ♐ 29 ♑	1 ♏	1 ♑ 24 ♒	1 ♏ 19 ♐	1 ♑ 8 ♒	1 ♐ 14 ♑	1 ♎ 7 ♏	1 ♑ 10 ♒

♀	1977	1978	1979	1980	1981	1982	1983	1984
JAN	1 ♒ 5 ♓	1 ♑ 21 ♒	1 ♏ 8 ♐	1 ♒ 16 ♓	1 ♐ 12 ♑	1 ♒ 24 ♑	1 ♑ 6 ♒ 30 ♓	1 ♏ 7 ♐ 26 ♑
FEB	1 ♓ 3 ♈	1 ♒ 14 ♓	1 ♐ 6 ♑	1 ♓ 10 ♈	1 ♑ 5 ♒ 28 ♓	1 ♑	1 ♓ 23 ♈	1 ♑ 20 ♒
MAR	1 ♈	1 ♓ 10 ♈	1 ♑ 4 ♒ 29 ♓	1 ♈ 25 ♉	1 ♓ 25 ♈	1 ♒	1 ♈ 20 ♉	1 ♒ 15 ♓
APR	1 ♈	1 ♈ 3 ♉ 28 ♊	1 ♓ 23 ♈	1 ♉ 4 ♊	1 ♈ 18 ♉	1 ♒ 7 ♓	1 ♉ 14 ♊	1 ♓ 8 ♈
MAY	1 ♈	1 ♊ 22 ♋	1 ♈ 18 ♉	1 ♊ 13 ♋	1 ♉ 12 ♊	1 ♓ 5 ♈	1 ♊ 10 ♋	1 ♈ 3 ♉ 27 ♊
JUN	1 ♈ 7 ♉	1 ♋ 17 ♌	1 ♉ 12 ♊	1 ♋ 6 ♊	1 ♊ 6 ♋ 30 ♌	1 ♉ 26 ♊	1 ♋ 7 ♌	1 ♊ 21 ♋
JUL	1 ♉ 7 ♊	1 ♌ 12 ♍	1 ♊ 7 ♋ 31 ♌	1 ♊	1 ♌ 25 ♍	1 ♊ 21 ♋	1 ♌ 11 ♍	1 ♋ 15 ♌
AUG	1 ♊ 3 ♋ 29 ♌	1 ♍ 7 ♎	1 ♌ 25 ♍	1 ♊ 8 ♋	1 ♍ 19 ♎	1 ♋ 15 ♌	1 ♍ 28 ♌	1 ♌ 8 ♍
SEP	1 ♌ 23 ♍	1 ♎ 8 ♏	1 ♍ 18 ♎	1 ♋ 8 ♌	1 ♎ 13 ♏	1 ♌ 8 ♍	1 ♌	1 ♍ 2 ♎ 26 ♏
OCT	1 ♍ 17 ♎	1 ♏	1 ♎ 12 ♏	1 ♌ 5 ♍ 31 ♎	1 ♏ 7 ♐	1 ♍ 2 ♎ 26 ♏	1 ♌ 6 ♍	1 ♏ 21 ♐
NOV	1 ♎ 11 ♏	1 ♏	1 ♏ 5 ♐ 29 ♑	1 ♎ 25 ♏	1 ♐ 6 ♑	1 ♏ 19 ♐	1 ♍ 10 ♎	1 ♐ 14 ♑
DEC	1 ♏ 4 ♐ 28 ♑	1 ♏	1 ♑ 23 ♒	1 ♏ 19 ♐	1 ♑ 9 ♒	1 ♐ 12 ♑	1 ♎ 7 ♏	1 ♑ 10 ♒

♀	1985	1986	1987	1988	1989	1990	1991	1992
JAN	1 ♒ 5 ♓	1 ♑ 21 ♒	1 ♏ 8 ♐	1 ♒ 16 ♓	1 ♐ 11 ♑	1 ♒ 17 ♑	1 ♑ 6 ♒ 30 ♓	1 ♐ 26 ♑
FEB	1 ♓ 3 ♈	1 ♒ 14 ♓	1 ♐ 6 ♑	1 ♒ 10 ♓	1 ♑ 4 ♒ 28 ♓	1 ♑	1 ♓ 23 ♈	1 ♑ 19 ♒
MAR	1 ♈	1 ♓ 9 ♈	1 ♑ 4 ♒ 29 ♓	1 ♈ 7 ♉	1 ♓ 24 ♈	1 ♑ 4 ♒	1 ♈ 8 ♉	1 ♒ 14 ♓
APR	1 ♈	1 ♈ 3 ♉ 27 ♊	1 ♓ 23 ♈	1 ♉ 4 ♊	1 ♈ 17 ♉	1 ♒ 7 ♓	1 ♉ 13 ♊	1 ♓ 7 ♈
MAY	1 ♈	1 ♊ 22 ♋	1 ♈ 18 ♉	1 ♊ 18 ♋ 27 ♊	1 ♉ 12 ♊	1 ♓ 4 ♈ 31 ♉	1 ♊ 9 ♋	1 ♈ 2 ♉ 26 ♊
JUN	1 ♈ 6 ♉	1 ♋ 16 ♌	1 ♉ 12 ♊	1 ♊	1 ♊ 5 ♋ 30 ♊	1 ♉ 25 ♊	1 ♋ 7 ♌	1 ♊ 20 ♋
JUL	1 ♉ 7 ♊	1 ♌ 12 ♍	1 ♊ 6 ♋ 31 ♌	1 ♊	1 ♋ 24 ♌	1 ♊ 20 ♋	1 ♌ 11 ♍	1 ♋ 14 ♌
AUG	1 ♊ 3 ♋ 28 ♌	1 ♍ 8 ♎	1 ♋ 24 ♌	1 ♊ 7 ♋	1 ♌ 18 ♍	1 ♋ 13 ♌	1 ♍ 22 ♎	1 ♌ 7 ♍
SEP	1 ♌ 23 ♍	1 ♎ 8 ♏	1 ♍ 17 ♎	1 ♌ 8 ♍	1 ♍ 13 ♎	1 ♌ 9 ♍	1 ♎	1 ♍ 25 ♎
OCT	1 ♍ 17 ♎	1 ♏	1 ♎ 11 ♏	1 ♌ 5 ♍ 30 ♎	1 ♏ 9 ♐	1 ♍ 2 ♎ 26 ♏	1 ♎	1 ♎ 20 ♏
NOV	1 ♎ 10 ♏	1 ♏	1 ♏ 4 ♐ 28 ♑	1 ♎ 24 ♏	1 ♐ 6 ♑	1 ♏ 19 ♐	1 ♎ 9 ♏	1 ♏ 14 ♐
DEC	1 ♏ 4 ♐ 28 ♑	1 ♏	1 ♑ 23 ♒	1 ♏ 18 ♐	1 ♑ 10 ♒	1 ♐ 13 ♑	1 ♏ 7 ♐	1 ♐ 9 ♑

♀	1993	1994	1995	1996	1997	1998	1999	2000
JAN	1 ♒ 4 ♓	1 ♑ 20 ♒	1 ♏ 8 ♐	1 ♒ 15 ♓	1 ♐ 10 ♑	1 ♒ 10 ♑	1 ♑ 5 ♒ 29 ♓	1 ♐ 25 ♑
FEB	1 ♓ 3 ♈	1 ♒ 13 ♓	1 ♐ 5 ♑	1 ♒ 9 ♓	1 ♑ 4 ♒ 28 ♓	1 ♑	1 ♓ 22 ♈	1 ♑ 19 ♒
MAR	1 ♈	1 ♓ 9 ♈	1 ♑ 3 ♒ 29 ♓	1 ♈ 6 ♉	1 ♓ 24 ♈	1 ♑ 5 ♒	1 ♈ 19 ♉	1 ♒ 14 ♓
APR	1 ♈	1 ♈ 2 ♉ 27 ♊	1 ♓ 23 ♈	1 ♉ 4 ♊	1 ♈ 17 ♉	1 ♒ 7 ♓	1 ♉ 13 ♊	1 ♓ 7 ♈
MAY	1 ♈	1 ♊ 21 ♋	1 ♈ 17 ♉	1 ♊	1 ♉ 11 ♊	1 ♓ 4 ♈ 30 ♉	1 ♊ 9 ♋	1 ♈ 2 ♉ 26 ♊
JUN	1 ♈ 7 ♉	1 ♋ 15 ♌	1 ♉ 11 ♊	1 ♊	1 ♊ 4 ♋ 29 ♊	1 ♉ 25 ♊	1 ♋ 6 ♌	1 ♊ 19 ♋
JUL	1 ♉ 6 ♊	1 ♌ 12 ♍	1 ♊ 6 ♋ 30 ♌	1 ♊	1 ♋ 24 ♌	1 ♊ 20 ♋	1 ♌ 13 ♍	1 ♋ 14 ♌
AUG	1 ♊ 2 ♋ 28 ♌	1 ♍ 8 ♎	1 ♋ 23 ♌	1 ♊ 8 ♋	1 ♌ 18 ♍	1 ♋ 14 ♌	1 ♍ 16 ♎	1 ♌ 7 ♍
SEP	1 ♌ 22 ♍	1 ♎ 8 ♏	1 ♍ 17 ♎	1 ♌ 8 ♍	1 ♍ 12 ♎	1 ♌ 7 ♍	1 ♎	1 ♍ 25 ♎
OCT	1 ♍ 16 ♎	1 ♏	1 ♎ 11 ♏	1 ♌ 5 ♍ 30 ♎	1 ♏ 9 ♐	1 ♍ 2 ♎ 26 ♏	1 ♎	1 ♎ 20 ♏
NOV	1 ♎ 9 ♏	1 ♏	1 ♏ 4 ♐ 28 ♑	1 ♎ 23 ♏	1 ♏ 6 ♐	1 ♏ 18 ♐	1 ♎ 10 ♏	1 ♏ 13 ♐
DEC	1 ♏ 3 ♐ 27 ♑	1 ♏	1 ♑ 22 ♒	1 ♏ 17 ♐	1 ♑ 12 ♒	1 ♐ 12 ♑	1 ♏ 6 ♐	1 ♐ 9 ♑

– MARS TABLES –

♂	1921	1922	1923	1924	1925	1926	1927	1928	1929	1930
JAN	1 ♒ 5 ♓	1 ♏	1 ♓ 21 ♈	1 ♏ 19 ♐	1 ♈	1 ♐	1 ♉	1 ♐ 19 ♑	1 ♊	1 ♑
FEB	1 ♓ 13 ♈	1 ♏ 18 ♐	1 ♈	1 ♐	1 ♈ 5 ♉	1 ♐ 9 ♑	1 ♉ 22 ♊	1 ♑ 28 ♒	1 ♊	1 ♑ 6 ♒
MAR	1 ♈ 25 ♉	1 ♐	1 ♈ 4 ♉	1 ♐ 6 ♑	1 ♉ 24 ♊	1 ♑ 23 ♒	1 ♊	1 ♒	1 ♊ 10 ♋	1 ♒ 17 ♓
APR	1 ♉	1 ♐	1 ♉ 16 ♊	1 ♑ 24 ♒	1 ♊	1 ♒	1 ♊ 17 ♋	1 ♒ 17 ♓	1 ♋	1 ♓ 24 ♈
MAY	1 ♉ 6 ♊	1 ♐	1 ♊ 30 ♋	1 ♒	1 ♊ 9 ♋	1 ♒ 3 ♓	1 ♋	1 ♓ 16 ♈	1 ♋ 13 ♌	1 ♈
JUN	1 ♊ 18 ♋	1 ♐	1 ♋	1 ♒ 24 ♓	1 ♋ 26 ♌	1 ♓ 14 ♈	1 ♋ 6 ♌	1 ♈ 26 ♉	1 ♌	1 ♈ 3 ♉
JUL	1 ♋	1 ♐	1 ♋ 16 ♌	1 ♓	1 ♌	1 ♈	1 ♌ 25 ♍	1 ♉	1 ♌ 4 ♍	1 ♉ 14 ♊
AUG	1 ♋ 3 ♌	1 ♐	1 ♌	1 ♓ 24 ♒	1 ♌ 24 ♍	1 ♈ 10 ♉	1 ♍	1 ♉ 9 ♊	1 ♍ 21 ♎	1 ♊ 28 ♋
SEP	1 ♌ 19 ♍	1 ♐ 13 ♑	1 ♍	1 ♒	1 ♍ 28 ♎	1 ♉	1 ♍ 10 ♎	1 ♊	1 ♎	1 ♋
OCT	1 ♍	1 ♑ 30 ♒	1 ♍ 18 ♎	1 ♒ 19 ♓	1 ♎	1 ♉	1 ♎ 26 ♏	1 ♊ 3 ♋	1 ♎ 6 ♏	1 ♋ 20 ♌
NOV	1 ♍ 6 ♎	1 ♒	1 ♎	1 ♓	1 ♎ 13 ♏	1 ♉	1 ♏	1 ♋	1 ♏ 18 ♐	1 ♌
DEC	1 ♎ 26 ♏	1 ♒ 11 ♓	1 ♎ 4 ♏	1 ♓ 19 ♈	1 ♏ 28 ♐	1 ♉	1 ♏ 8 ♐	1 ♋ 20 ♊	1 ♐ 29 ♑	1 ♌

♂	1931	1932	1933	1934	1935	1936	1937	1938	1939	1940
JAN	1 ♌	1 ♑ 18 ♒	1 ♍	1 ♒	1 ♎	1 ♒ 14 ♓	1 ♍ 5 ♎	1 ♓ 30 ♈	1 ♏ 29 ♐	1 ♓ 4 ♈
FEB	1 ♌ 16 ♋	1 ♒ 25 ♓	1 ♍	1 ♒ 4 ♓	1 ♎	1 ♓ 22 ♈	1 ♎	1 ♈	1 ♐	1 ♈ 17 ♉
MAR	1 ♋ 30 ♌	1 ♓	1 ♍	1 ♓ 14 ♈	1 ♎	1 ♈	1 ♎ 13 ♏	1 ♈ 12 ♉	1 ♐ 21 ♑	1 ♉
APR	1 ♌	1 ♓ 3 ♈	1 ♍	1 ♈ 22 ♉	1 ♎	1 ♈	1 ♏	1 ♉ 23 ♊	1 ♑	1 ♊
MAY	1 ♌	1 ♈ 12 ♉	1 ♍	1 ♉	1 ♎	1 ♈ 13 ♉	1 ♏	1 ♊	1 ♑ 25 ♒	1 ♊ 17 ♋
JUN	1 ♌ 10 ♍	1 ♉ 22 ♊	1 ♍	1 ♉ 2 ♊	1 ♎	1 ♉ 25 ♊	1 ♏	1 ♊ 7 ♋	1 ♒	1 ♋
JUL	1 ♍	1 ♊	1 ♍ 6 ♎	1 ♊ 15 ♋	1 ♎ 29 ♏	1 ♊	1 ♏	1 ♋ 22 ♌	1 ♒ 21 ♑	1 ♋ 3 ♌
AUG	1 ♎	1 ♊ 4 ♋	1 ♎ 26 ♏	1 ♋ 30 ♌	1 ♏	1 ♊ 10 ♋	1 ♏ 8 ♐	1 ♌	1 ♑	1 ♌ 19 ♍
SEP	1 ♎ 17 ♏	1 ♋ 20 ♌	1 ♏	1 ♌	1 ♏ 16 ♐	1 ♋ 26 ♌	1 ♐	1 ♌ 7 ♍	1 ♑ 24 ♒	1 ♍
OCT	1 ♏ 30 ♐	1 ♌	1 ♏ 9 ♐	1 ♌ 18 ♍	1 ♐ 28 ♑	1 ♌	1 ♐ 30 ♑	1 ♍ 25 ♎	1 ♒	1 ♍ 5 ♎
NOV	1 ♐	1 ♌ 13 ♍	1 ♐ 19 ♑	1 ♍	1 ♑	1 ♌ 14 ♍	1 ♑	1 ♎	1 ♒ 19 ♓	1 ♎ 20 ♏
DEC	1 ♐ 10 ♑	1 ♍	1 ♑ 28 ♒	1 ♍ 11 ♎	1 ♑ 7 ♒	1 ♍	1 ♒	1 ♎ 11 ♏	1 ♓	1 ♏

– MARS TABLES –

♂	1941	1942	1943	1944	1945	1946	1947	1948	1949	1950
JAN	1♏ 4♐	1♈ 11♉	1♐ 26♑	1♊	1♐ 5♑	1♋	1♑ 25♒	1♍	1♑ 4♒	1♎
FEB	1♐ 17♑	1♉	1♑	1♊	1♑ 14♒	1♋	1♒	1♍ 12♌	1♒ 11♓	1♎
MAR	1♑	1♉ 7♊	1♑ 8♒	1♊ 29♋	1♒ 25♓	1♋	1♒ 4♓	1♌	1♓ 21♈	1♎ 28♍
APR	1♑ 2♒	1♊ 26♋	1♒ 17♓	1♋	1♓	1♋ 22♌	1♓ 11♈	1♌	1♈ 30♉	1♍
MAY	1♒ 16♓	1♋	1♓ 27♈	1♋ 22♌	1♓ 3♈	1♌	1♈ 21♉	1♌ 18♍	1♉	1♍
JUN	1♓	1♋ 14♌	1♈	1♌	1♈ 11♉	1♌ 20♍	1♉	1♍	1♉ 10♊	1♍ 11♎
JUL	1♓ 2♈	1♌	1♈ 7♉	1♌ 12♍	1♉ 23♊	1♍	1♊	1♍ 17♎	1♊ 23♋	1♎
AUG	1♈	1♍	1♉ 23♊	1♍ 29♎	1♊	1♍ 9♎	1♊ 13♋	1♎	1♋	1♎ 10♏
SEP	1♈	1♍ 17♎	1♊	1♎	1♊ 7♋	1♎ 24♏	1♋	1♎ 3♏	1♋ 7♌	1♏ 25♐
OCT	1♈	1♎	1♊	1♎ 13♏	1♋	1♏	1♌	1♏ 17♐	1♌ 27♍	1♐
NOV	1♈	1♎ 2♏	1♊	1♏ 25♐	1♋ 11♌	1♏ 6♐	1♌	1♐ 26♑	1♍	1♐ 6♑
DEC	1♈	1♏ 15♐	1♊	1♐	1♌ 26♋	1♐ 17♑	1♍	1♑	1♍ 26♎	1♑ 15♒

♂	1951	1952	1953	1954	1955	1956	1957	1958	1959	1960
JAN	1♒ 22♓	1♎ 20♏	1♓	1♏	1♓ 15♈	1♏ 14♐	1♈ 28♉	1♐	1♉	1♐ 14♑
FEB	1♓	1♏	1♓ 8♈	1♏ 9♐	1♈ 26♉	1♐ 28♑	1♉	1♐ 3♑	1♉ 10♊	1♑ 23♒
MAR	1♓ 2♈	1♏	1♈ 20♉	1♐	1♉	1♑	1♉ 17♊	1♑ 17♒	1♊	1♒
APR	1♈ 10♉	1♏	1♉	1♐ 12♑	1♉ 10♊	1♑ 14♒	1♊	1♒ 27♓	1♊ 10♋	1♒ 2♓
MAY	1♉ 21♊	1♏	1♊	1♑	1♊ 26♋	1♒	1♊ 4♋	1♓	1♋	1♓ 11♈
JUN	1♊	1♏	1♊ 14♋	1♑	1♋	1♒ 3♓	1♋ 21♌	1♓ 7♈	1♋ 2♌	1♈ 20♉
JUL	1♊ 3♋	1♏	1♋ 29♌	1♑	1♋ 11♌	1♓	1♌	1♈ 21♉	1♌ 20♍	1♉
AUG	1♋ 18♌	1♏ 27♐	1♌	1♑	1♌ 27♍	1♓	1♌ 8♍	1♉	1♍	1♉ 2♊
SEP	1♌	1♐	1♌ 14♍	1♑	1♍	1♓	1♍ 24♎	1♉ 21♊	1♍ 5♎	1♊ 21♋
OCT	1♌ 5♍	1♐ 12♑	1♍	1♑ 21♒	1♍ 13♎	1♓	1♎	1♊ 29♉	1♎ 21♏	1♋
NOV	1♍ 24♎	1♑ 21♒	1♎	1♒	1♎ 29♏	1♓	1♎ 8♏	1♉	1♏	1♋
DEC	1♎	1♒ 30♓	1♎ 20♏	1♒ 4♓	1♏	1♓ 6♈	1♏ 23♐	1♉	1♏ 3♐	1♋

– MARS TABLES –

♂	1961	1962	1963	1964	1965	1966	1967	1968	1969	1970
JAN	1 ♋	1 ♑	1 ♌	1 ♑ · 13 ♒	1 ♍	1 ♒ · 30 ♓	1 ♎	1 ♒ · 9 ♓	1 ♏	1 ♓ · 24 ♈
FEB	1 ♋ · 5 ♊ · 7 ♋	1 ♑ · 2 ♒	1 ♌	1 ♒ · 20 ♓	1 ♍	1 ♓	1 ♎ · 12 ♏	1 ♓ · 17 ♈	1 ♏ · 25 ♐	1 ♈
MAR	1 ♋	1 ♒ · 12 ♓	1 ♌	1 ♓ · 29 ♈	1 ♍	1 ♓ · 9 ♈	1 ♏ · 31 ♎	1 ♈ · 27 ♉	1 ♐	1 ♈ · 7 ♉
APR	1 ♋	1 ♓ · 19 ♈	1 ♌	1 ♈	1 ♍	1 ♈ · 17 ♉	1 ♎	1 ♉	1 ♐	1 ♉ · 18 ♊
MAY	1 ♋ · 6 ♌	1 ♈ · 28 ♉	1 ♌	1 ♈ · 7 ♉	1 ♍	1 ♉ · 28 ♊	1 ♎	1 ♉ · 8 ♊	1 ♐	1 ♊
JUN	1 ♌ · 28 ♍	1 ♉	1 ♌ · 3 ♍	1 ♉ · 17 ♊	1 ♍ · 29 ♎	1 ♊	1 ♎	1 ♊ · 21 ♋	1 ♐	1 ♊ · 2 ♋
JUL	1 ♍	1 ♉ · 9 ♊	1 ♍ · 27 ♎	1 ♊ · 30 ♋	1 ♎	1 ♊ · 11 ♋	1 ♎ · 19 ♏	1 ♋	1 ♐	1 ♋ · 18 ♌
AUG	1 ♍ · 17 ♎	1 ♊ · 22 ♋	1 ♎	1 ♋	1 ♎ · 20 ♏	1 ♋ · 25 ♌	1 ♏	1 ♋ · 5 ♌	1 ♐	1 ♌
SEP	1 ♎	1 ♋	1 ♎ · 12 ♏	1 ♋ · 15 ♌	1 ♏	1 ♌	1 ♏ · 10 ♐	1 ♌ · 21 ♍	1 ♐ · 21 ♑	1 ♌ · 3 ♍
OCT	1 ♎ · 2 ♏	1 ♋ · 11 ♌	1 ♏ · 25 ♐	1 ♌	1 ♏ · 4 ♐	1 ♌ · 12 ♍	1 ♐ · 23 ♑	1 ♍	1 ♑	1 ♍ · 20 ♎
NOV	1 ♏ · 13 ♐	1 ♌	1 ♐	1 ♌ · 6 ♍	1 ♐ · 14 ♑	1 ♍	1 ♑	1 ♍ · 9 ♎	1 ♑ · 4 ♒	1 ♎
DEC	1 ♐ · 24 ♑	1 ♌	1 ♐ · 5 ♑	1 ♍	1 ♑ · 23 ♒	1 ♍ · 4 ♎	1 ♑ · 2 ♒	1 ♎ · 29 ♏	1 ♒ · 15 ♓	1 ♎ · 6 ♏

♂	1971	1972	1973	1974	1975	1976	1977	1978	1979	1980
JAN	1 ♏ · 23 ♐	1 ♈	1 ♐	1 ♉	1 ♐ · 21 ♑	1 ♊	1 ♐	1 ♌ · 26 ♋	1 ♑ · 20 ♒	1 ♍
FEB	1 ♐	1 ♈ · 10 ♉	1 ♐ · 12 ♑	1 ♉ · 27 ♊	1 ♑	1 ♊	1 ♐ · 9 ♑	1 ♋	1 ♒ · 27 ♓	1 ♍
MAR	1 ♐ · 12 ♑	1 ♉ · 27 ♊	1 ♑ · 27 ♒	1 ♊	1 ♑ · 3 ♒	1 ♊ · 18 ♋	1 ♑ · 20 ♒	1 ♋	1 ♓	1 ♍ · 12 ♌
APR	1 ♑	1 ♊	1 ♒	1 ♊ · 20 ♋	1 ♒ · 11 ♓	1 ♋	1 ♒ · 27 ♓	1 ♋ · 11 ♌	1 ♓ · 7 ♈	1 ♌
MAY	1 ♑ · 3 ♒	1 ♊ · 12 ♋	1 ♒ · 8 ♓	1 ♋	1 ♓ · 21 ♈	1 ♋ · 16 ♌	1 ♓	1 ♌	1 ♈ · 16 ♉	1 ♌ · 4 ♍
JUN	1 ♒	1 ♋ · 28 ♌	1 ♓ · 20 ♈	1 ♋ · 9 ♌	1 ♈	1 ♌	1 ♓ · 6 ♈	1 ♌ · 14 ♍	1 ♉ · 26 ♊	1 ♍
JUL	1 ♒	1 ♌	1 ♈	1 ♌ · 27 ♍	1 ♉	1 ♌ · 6 ♍	1 ♈ · 17 ♉	1 ♍	1 ♊	1 ♍ · 11 ♎
AUG	1 ♒	1 ♌ · 15 ♍	1 ♈ · 12 ♉	1 ♍	1 ♉ · 14 ♊	1 ♍ · 24 ♎	1 ♉	1 ♍ · 4 ♎	1 ♊ · 8 ♋	1 ♎ · 29 ♏
SEP	1 ♒	1 ♍	1 ♉	1 ♍ · 12 ♎	1 ♊	1 ♎	1 ♊	1 ♎ · 19 ♏	1 ♋ · 24 ♌	1 ♏
OCT	1 ♒	1 ♎	1 ♉ · 30 ♈	1 ♎ · 28 ♏	1 ♊	1 ♎ · 8 ♏	1 ♊ · 26 ♋	1 ♏	1 ♌	1 ♏ · 12 ♐
NOV	1 ♒ · 6 ♓	1 ♎ · 15 ♏	1 ♈	1 ♏	1 ♊	1 ♏ · 20 ♐	1 ♋	1 ♏ · 2 ♐	1 ♌ · 19 ♍	1 ♐ · 22 ♑
DEC	1 ♓ · 26 ♈	1 ♏ · 30 ♐	1 ♈ · 24 ♉	1 ♏ · 10 ♐	1 ♊	1 ♐	1 ♋ · 27 ♌	1 ♐ · 12 ♑	1 ♍	1 ♑ · 31 ♒

– MARS TABLES –

♂	1981	1982	1983	1984	1985	1986	1987	1988	1989	1990
JAN	1 ♒	1 ♎	1 ♒ 17 ♓	1 ♎ 11 ♏	1 ♓	1 ♏	1 ♓ 8 ♈	1 ♏ ♐	1 ♈ 19 ♉	1 ♐ 30 ♑
FEB	1 ♒ 7 ♓	1 ♎	1 ♓ 25 ♈	1 ♏	1 ♓ 3 ♈	1 ♏ 2 ♐	1 ♈ 21 ♉	1 ♐ 22 ♑	1 ♉	1 ♑
MAR	1 ♓ 17 ♈	1 ♎	1 ♈	1 ♏	1 ♈ 15 ♉	1 ♐ 28 ♑	1 ♉	1 ♑	1 ♉ 11 ♊	1 ♑ 12 ♒
APR	1 ♈ 25 ♉	1 ♎	1 ♈ 5 ♉	1 ♏	1 ♉ 26 ♊	1 ♑	1 ♉ 6 ♊	1 ♑ 7 ♒	1 ♊ 29 ♋	1 ♒ 21 ♓
MAY	1 ♉	1 ♎	1 ♉ 17 ♊	1 ♏	1 ♊	1 ♑	1 ♊ 21 ♋	1 ♒ 22 ♓	1 ♋	1 ♓ 31 ♈
JUN	1 ♉ 5 ♊	1 ♎	1 ♊ 29 ♋	1 ♏	1 ♊ 9 ♋	1 ♑	1 ♋	1 ♓	1 ♋ 17 ♌	1 ♈
JUL	1 ♊ 18 ♋	1 ♎	1 ♋	1 ♏	1 ♋ 25 ♌	1 ♑	1 ♋ 7 ♌	1 ♓ 14 ♈	1 ♌	1 ♈ 13 ♉
AUG	1 ♋	1 ♎ 3 ♏	1 ♋ 14 ♌	1 ♏ 18 ♐	1 ♌	1 ♑	1 ♌ 23 ♍	1 ♈	1 ♌ 3 ♍	1 ♉ 31 ♊
SEP	1 ♋ 2 ♌	1 ♏ 20 ♐	1 ♌ 30 ♍	1 ♐	1 ♌ 10 ♍	1 ♑	1 ♍	1 ♈	1 ♍ 20 ♎	1 ♊
OCT	1 ♌ 21 ♍	1 ♐	1 ♍	1 ♐ 5 ♑	1 ♍ 28 ♎	1 ♑ 9 ♒	1 ♍ 9 ♎	1 ♈ 24 ♓	1 ♎	1 ♊
NOV	1 ♍	1 ♑	1 ♍ 18 ♎	1 ♑ 16 ♒	1 ♎	1 ♒ 26 ♓	1 ♎ 24 ♏	1 ♈ 2 ♓	1 ♎ 4 ♏	1 ♊
DEC	1 ♍ 16 ♎	1 ♑ 10 ♒	1 ♎	1 ♒ 25 ♓	1 ♎ 15 ♏	1 ♓	1 ♏	1 ♈	1 ♏ 18 ♐	1 ♊ 14 ♉

♂	1991	1992	1993	1994	1995	1996	1997	1998	1999	2000
JAN	1 ♉ 21 ♊	1 ♐ 9 ♑	1 ♋	1 ♑ 28 ♒	1 ♌ 23 ♋	1 ♑ 9 ♒	1 ♍ 3 ♎	1 ♑ 25 ♒	1 ♎ 26 ♏	1 ♒ 4 ♓
FEB	1 ♊	1 ♑ 18 ♒	1 ♋	1 ♒	1 ♌	1 ♒ 15 ♓	1 ♎	1 ♓	1 ♏	1 ♓ 12 ♈
MAR	1 ♊	1 ♒ 28 ♓	1 ♋	1 ♓ 7 ♈	1 ♌	1 ♓ 25 ♈	1 ♎ 9 ♍	1 ♓ 5 ♈	1 ♏	1 ♈ 23 ♉
APR	1 ♊ 3 ♋	1 ♓	1 ♋ 28 ♌	1 ♈ 15 ♉	1 ♌	1 ♈	1 ♍	1 ♈ 13 ♉	1 ♏	1 ♉
MAY	1 ♋ 27 ♌	1 ♓ 6 ♈	1 ♌	1 ♉ 24 ♊	1 ♌ 26 ♍	1 ♈ 3 ♉	1 ♍	1 ♉ 24 ♊	1 ♏ 6 ♎	1 ♉ 4 ♊
JUN	1 ♌	1 ♈ 15 ♉	1 ♌ 23 ♍	1 ♊	1 ♍	1 ♉ 12 ♊	1 ♍ 19 ♎	1 ♊	1 ♎	1 ♊ 16 ♋
JUL	1 ♌ 16 ♍	1 ♉ 27 ♊	1 ♍	1 ♉ 4 ♊	1 ♍ 21 ♎	1 ♊ 26 ♋	1 ♎	1 ♊ 6 ♋	1 ♎ 5 ♏	1 ♋
AUG	1 ♍	1 ♊	1 ♍ 12 ♎	1 ♊ 17 ♋	1 ♎	1 ♋	1 ♎ 14 ♏	1 ♋ 21 ♌	1 ♏	1 ♌
SEP	1 ♎	1 ♊ 12 ♋	1 ♎ 27 ♏	1 ♋	1 ♎ 7 ♏	1 ♋ 10 ♌	1 ♏ 29 ♐	1 ♌	1 ♏ 3 ♐	1 ♌ 17 ♍
OCT	1 ♎ 17 ♏	1 ♋	1 ♏	1 ♋ 5 ♌	1 ♏ 21 ♐	1 ♌ 30 ♍	1 ♐	1 ♌ 7 ♍	1 ♐ 17 ♑	1 ♍
NOV	1 ♏ 29 ♐	1 ♋	1 ♏ 9 ♐	1 ♌	1 ♐	1 ♍	1 ♐ 9 ♑	1 ♍ 27 ♎	1 ♑ 26 ♒	1 ♍ 4 ♎
DEC	1 ♐	1 ♋	1 ♐ 20 ♑	1 ♌ 12 ♍	1 ♑	1 ♍	1 ♑ 18 ♒	1 ♎	1 ♒	1 ♎ 23 ♏

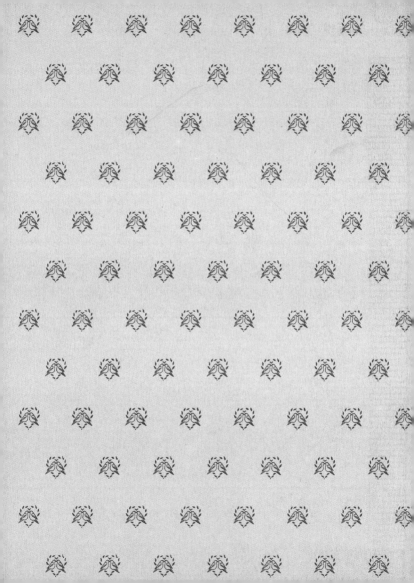